Someone Came Before You

by Pat Schwiebert
illustrated by Taylor Bills

Grief Watch
Portland, Oregon

THERE ONCE WAS A MOMMY AND A DADDY WHO LOVED
EACH OTHER VERY MUCH.

THEY LOVED TO RIDE BIKES AND DANCE AND WATCH TV
AND EVEN DO CHORES TOGETHER.

BUT THEY KNEW SOMETHING WAS MISSING.

THEY KNEW WHAT WAS MISSING WASN'T A CAT OR A DOG OR A BIRD OR A HAMSTER. THEY KNEW IT WASN'T A NEW CAR OR A NEW TV.

THEY KNEW THEY WANTED TO SHARE THEIR LIFE WITH
SOMEONE VERY SPECIAL.

THEY WANTED A BABY THAT WOULD GROW INTO A LITTLE PERSON WHO WOULD ALSO LOVE TO RIDE BIKES AND DANCE AND EVEN DO CHORES WITH THEM.

THEY WERE SO EXCITED WHEN THEY REALIZED THIS SPECIAL PERSON
WAS ON THE WAY.

THEY HEARD THEIR BABY AND FELT THEIR BABY AND WATCHED THEIR BABY GROW. THIS WAS TO BE A VERY SPECIAL BABY.

AND THE MOMMY WOULD
SIT IN THE ROCKER AND
SING TO HER BABY,
"BABY, I'M WAITING FOR YOU.
PRAYING FOR YOU.
DREAMING OF YOU.
AND WHEN ANOTHER DAY IS
THROUGH I'LL STILL BE
WAITING FOR YOU."

THEY LOVED THEIR SPECIAL BABY VERY MUCH.

BUT THINGS DIDN'T GO AS THEY HAD PLANNED.
THEIR VERY SPECIAL BABY DIED.

THE MOMMY AND DADDY MISSED THEIR SPECIAL BABY VERY MUCH.
THEY CRIED AND CRIED AND WERE SAD A WHOLE LOT.

AND THE MOMMY SANG AS
SHE SAT IN THE ROCKER,
"BABY, WE REMEMBER YOU.
THINK OF YOU.
PRAY FOR YOU.
AND WHEN ANOTHER DAY
IS THROUGH WE'LL STILL
REMEMBER YOU."

NOTHING WOULD MAKE THEM HAPPY.

AND SO THEIR HEARTS GREW VERY SMALL. NOTHING COULD GET IN.
NOTHING SEEMED TO MATTER. THEY DIDN'T WANT TO RIDE THEIR BIKES
OR DANCE OR EVEN DO THEIR CHORES. THEY JUST WANTED THEIR BABY.

EVEN THOUGH THE SPECIAL BABY DIED, THE BABY KEPT LOVING THE MOMMY
AND DADDY AND TRIED TO MAKE THEM HAPPY AGAIN.

THEIR SPECIAL BABY WAS VERY
PATIENT. AND THE SPECIAL
BABY WOULD SING,
"MOMMY, I REMEMBER YOU.
THINK OF YOU.
PRAY FOR YOU.
AND WHEN ANOTHER DAY
IS THROUGH I STILL
REMEMBER YOU."

FINALLY AFTER WHAT SEEMED LIKE MUCH WORK ON THE SPECIAL BABY'S PART, THE MOMMY AND DADDY'S HEARTS WERE STRETCHED BIG ENOUGH TO LET IN MORE LOVE.

AND NOW THERE WAS ROOM ENOUGH FOR ANOTHER SPECIAL BABY TO COME INTO THEIR HEARTS...AND THAT SPECIAL BABY IS YOU.

WE STILL THINK OF THAT SPECIAL SOMEONE WHO CAME BEFORE YOU.
WE HANG THE BABY'S ORNAMENT ON THE TREE NEXT TO YOURS.

AND WE HAVE A LITTLE BOX THAT WE PULL OUT FROM TIME TO TIME THAT HOLDS MEMORIES OF THAT SPECIAL BABY.

AND SOMETIMES WE LIGHT A CANDLE FOR THE BABY AND THANK THE BABY FOR STRETCHING OUR HEARTS TO MAKE ROOM FOR YOU.

Keeping Your Baby's Memory Alive

- It is quite natural for children to want to know the story of their family. Am I the oldest? Why is there only me? Why did you choose this name for me? Did someone come before me?

- As a way of remembering the family story, many families now have pictures of their dead baby displayed with other family portraits so that even before the child can talk the parent is introducing the child to everyone in the photos including that someone who came before them but died too soon.

- The result may be that, as the younger children grow they will feel a connection too, and may even include the baby in pictures they draw at school, or when reporting the number of siblings they have, when asked.

- But it is important to remember that this is your grief, not theirs. Your younger children will receive the story about a brother or sister who died only as a part of the family story, not as a reason for them also to experience sorrow or grief. They don't have the experience of a life with the baby in this world.

- Obviously, though, if you have older children who knew you were pregnant and went through the grieving process with you, their relationship to the dead baby will be different than for those who came after.

- Everyone has a personal story, even a baby who lived for only a short time. As that child's parent you have the privilege and opportunity to create the story from your memories, your hopes and dreams for that special person. Things you recall that you did while pregnant. Foods you liked or didn't like. Funny things you remember happening.

- And you can invite your other children to add to the story by talking about the ways the baby is in your family story now. So tell the baby's story. From time to time pull out the baby's memory box that contains special keepsakes. Show pictures, clothes, a blanket, a lock of hair, a rattle. These are all ways to make this baby real to the younger siblings.

- If you pray out loud as a family, include the baby's name. Hang an ornament for the holiday that displays the baby's name. Plant a tree, light a candle, or buy a gift for another child in memory of the one who died.

- Some people like to think of the baby as a new star in the heavens, so that "wishing on a star" becomes a way of maintaining a personal connection with that child.

- By showing your children you are not afraid to talk about death you are helping them develop healthy attitudes about death. Encourage them to ask questions and in return, ask them what they think. When you are sad, acknowledge that, but try not to dwell on the sadness. It's okay to look back. But don't stare. Let them see that you celebrate the life of the child who is gone. It's up to you to present this baby as worth remembering.

- A word of caution: sometimes bereaved parents develop unrealistic fantasies about their child who has died. The dead child becomes the perfect child, but only because he or she did not live long enough to do the things children do that drive parents up the wall! Be careful that you do not inadvertently communicate to surviving or subsequent siblings that you think they can somehow never measure up to the imagined flawlessness of this child who "should have lived."

We are glad you were here
and are with us still.

Additional Resources From Grief Watch

We We're Gonna Have A Baby, but We Had an Angel Instead by Pat Schwiebert Illustrated by Taylor Bills
A illustrated family book told from a young child's perspective about the excitement and plans for the coming baby, and the disappointment and sadness following the death of the baby.

Born To Fly by Cindy Claussen
This is one of those little treasures that will both touch and enlighten you as you absorb its powerful, yet simple, message.

The Angel with the Golden Glow by Ellissa Al-Chokhachy and illustrated by Ulrike Graf
A profound book of hope and healing for families who have lost a child or who have a child born special.

Memory Candle - lights of remembrance
A traditional cathedral candle with a quote printed on the front.
Four quotes to choose from, i.e. "Some people only dream of angels. We held one in our arms."